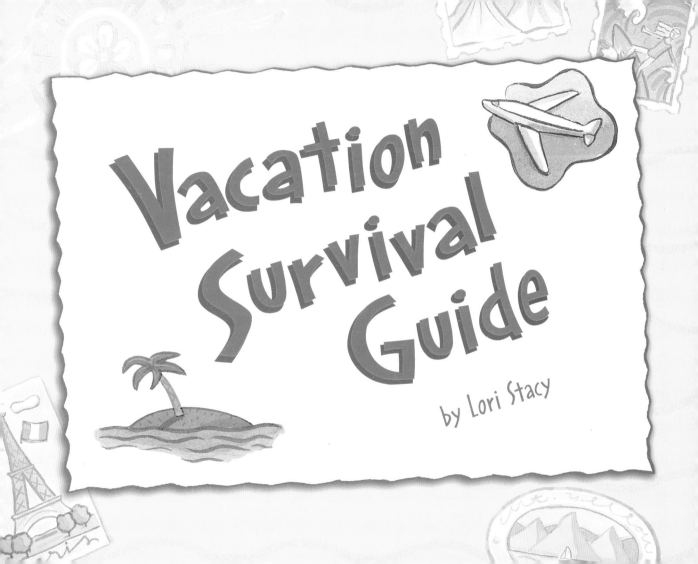

Vacation Survival Guide

by Lori Stacy

ISBN 0-439-24389-0

Illustrations by Maj Hagsted

Design by Julie Mullarkey

12 11 10 9 8 7 6 5 4 3 2 1   1 2 3 4 5 6/0

Printed in China
First Scholastic printing, April 2001

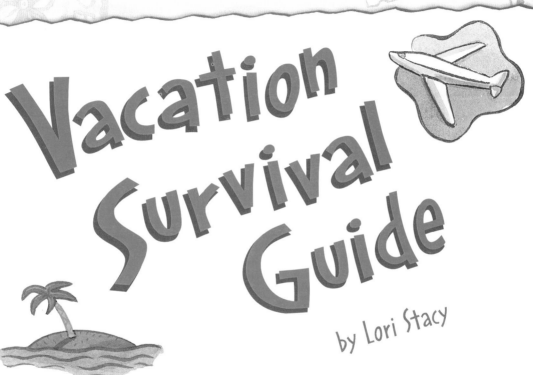

Vacation Survival Guide

by Lori Stacy

Scholastic Inc.

New York   Toronto   London   Auckland   Sydney   Mexico City   New Delhi   Hong Kong

Table of Contents

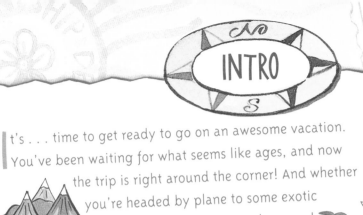

It's . . . time to get ready to go on an awesome vacation. You've been waiting for what seems like ages, and now the trip is right around the corner! And whether you're headed by plane to some exotic location or getting set to take a road trip to a relative's house, you can make this vacation your best ever.

This book is loaded with ideas to make the journey to your destination loads of fun. You'll find ways to beat backseat boredom and cure the what-to-do blues, and get great ideas for keeping in touch with the gang back home. You'll also get suggestions on how to collect and save special memories once you've returned from your trip, as well as a fab fill-in section to record your adventures. So get ready—the fun is about to begin . . . just don't forget to pack this book!

SUMMER CAMP SPECIAL:

Calling all campers!

If summer camp is where you're headed, be on the lookout for these helpful hints throughout the book to make camp an even more memorable experience.

Part 1

Travel Time: Planning and Packing

If you're super-excited about your vacation but it's still weeks or even months away, don't despair! There's a ton of fun stuff you can do to prepare, long before it's time to pack up and go. In fact, you'll find that planning and packing can be just as exciting!

Destination Investigation

If you're headed off into areas unknown, why not do a little research on your vacation destination? Learning more about where it is you're headed will not only provide you with the scoop on your vacation spot, but will also get you even more excited about visiting. Check out the Web or your local bookstore and see what you can dig up.

Another thing to do beforehand is to identify the places you'd love to visit or the things you'd like to do once you're there. Find out if there are any special shows or festivals taking place during your stay, and see if there are places that offer activities for kids your age. If you'll be traveling by car, you can also do some sleuthing to find neat places to stop for sight seeing during your journey.

TRAVEL TIP

Traveling with a pal can make your vacation even more adventurous. So why not ask your folks if you can bring along a bud on your next family vacation to share the fun memories with firsthand? (And if you *can't* take a friend on the trip, be sure to take lots of pictures so you can share them with her when you get home.)

Hot Spots

A lot of thought goes into planning the perfect family vacation or holiday trip. No doubt your folks want to make this fun for everyone. They might even ask for your opinion on where you'd love to spend your next vacation. Stumped on spots that would be fun for you and the fam? Here are some suggestions for great trips to take.

 Visit a National Park. There are more than 350 national parks in the United States, ranging from the vast wilderness of Yellowstone National Park in Wyoming and Yosemite National Park in California to historic monuments like Gettysburg National Park in Pennsylvania.

Go on an Island Adventure. Head to Hawaii, the Caribbean, or the Florida Keys for water activities and a great view of the ocean.

Camp Out. Get close to nature by heading into the wilderness for a camping or hiking vacation.

 Do a Disney Vacation. Head to either Walt Disney World in Florida or Disneyland in California for an amusement-filled holiday.

 See the Nation's Capital. Visit Washington, D.C., and get an up-close look at the White House and the Capitol Building, and stop in at the many great museums, such as the Smithsonian, that line the National Mall.

Roadside Oddities

Want to see something you'll never forget? Check out these curiosities while you're on the road.

Claude Bell's Dinosaurs — California (Cabazon, off I-10): These giant dinosaurs have been featured in movies, music videos, and even a Coke commercial. A small museum inside one of the dinos' tummies sells prehistoric-themed souvenirs.

The Largest Wooden Indian in the World — Maine (Skowhegan, US-201 at US-2): Though it stands in a parking lot behind a gas station, you won't miss this wooden statue—it's 62 feet high!

Mystery Spot — California (Santa Cruz, Hwy-1 at Branciforte Drive): Unusual things happen at this spot in the redwood forest . . . like balls rolling uphill and trees growing in strange shapes.

North Dakota's Roadside Giants — Driving through North Dakota, you're sure to see at least one of these giant sculptures: World's Largest Buffalo (Jamestown, I-90); World's Largest Turtle (Bottineau, Hwy-5); and World's Largest Cow (New Salem, I-94).

Prairie Dog Town — Kansas (Oakley, off US-83): A combo petting zoo and unique animal show, there are collections of prairie dogs as well as other critters from this part of the country. There's even a six-legged cow.

Lucy the Elephant — New Jersey (Margate, south of Atlantic City): This six-story-high elephant, made of wood and tin, houses a small museum of local history. And up on Lucy's back, you can get a view of the town.

The Thing — Arizona (Highway I-10 at exit 322): If you're driving along I-10 in Arizona, you probably won't be able to miss all the road signs advertising "The Thing," a combo gas station, gift shop, and fast-food restaurant that houses a shed full of oddities!

Wigwam Motel — California (San Bernardino, old Route 66): The rooms in this roadside motel are actually concrete teepees!

The World's Largest Man-made Star — Virginia (Roanoke, on Mill Mountain): This 100-foot-tall star shines bright every night, lit by 2,000 feet of neon tubing.

World's Largest Catsup Bottle — Illinois (Collinsville, Hwy. 159): This 170-foot-high catsup bottle, on the grounds of a former catsup company, will leave you longing for a big, juicy burger!

Vacation Survival 101

Traveling is exciting, that's for sure. But amid all the excitement can come the potential for trouble. Being overly tired, adjusting to new surroundings, or even just being stuck in the car for long periods of time can sometimes add tension to your travels. Here are some tips to consider before the trip that can help you prevent and survive vacation stress.

TRAVEL TIP

If you're on a sports team or take classes of some sort, you'll want to clue in your coaches or instructors to when you'll be away.

1 Schedule some solo time. Everybody needs a little alone time, especially when you're traveling and spending every waking moment of the day together. Leave blocks of time when you can read, do puzzles, or make crafts on your own for that much-needed time-out.

TRAVEL TIP

If you're going to stay with relatives or friends, think about bringing along a host gift from your hometown. Consider something that they may not be able to get in their part of the country, such as a special food or a craft that's related to where you live. Not only will your hosts appreciate the gesture, but you'll also be able to share a little of your hometown with them as you enjoy theirs.

2 Don't let hunger or exhaustion turn you into the travel beast. Vacations mean staying up later than usual, not always eating dinner at six, and other schedule busters that can create crankiness among you and your family. Be aware of your food moods and sleepy stress, and don't let it get the best of you!

3 Go easy on the itinerary. Don't try to pack too much into one day. If, for instance, you have a big morning of sight seeing planned, leave the afternoon open for something relaxing, like hanging out at the pool or by the beach.

Summer Camp Special:

Heading back to the same camp this year? Get out your address book from last year and send your camp pals a postcard or e-mail. To make your reunion even more exciting, suggest that you all wear the same stand-out clothes the first day of camp, like a red tank with denim shorts.

Gear to Get You There

So you know *where* you're going, but *what* are you going to bring? First of all, whether you're traveling by plane, train, or car, it's always a good idea to tote a carry-on bag that you keep with you. In it, you can pack stuff to entertain yourself, along with other must-haves for the trip, such as:

A deck of cards — You can help beat the "are we there yet?" blues by playing card games or, if you're traveling solo, a game of solitaire.

Your favorite music — Make a tape of your favorite tunes and bring your headset to play 'em in.

Good reads — Be sure to bring along one or two books (including this one!), as well as fun magazines to make the trip more enjoyable.

Your pillow — Sleeping in new places, like the backseat of the car, a plane seat that barely reclines, or a strange hotel bed, can leave you longing for the comforts of home. And while you can't pack your mattress, you *can* bring along your pillow to rest a little easier.

Snack packs — Bring along snacks for your trip. After all, you won't be able to breeze into the kitchen to squelch a snack attack while you're on a plane or in a car! Pack fruit, water bottles, and small bags of nuts, or peanut butter and crackers. Another good munchie to bring along: a bag of homemade trail mix. Try the easy-to-make recipe on the next page!

TRAVEL TIP

To make your luggage stand out from the crowd, try tying a colorful ribbon to the handle, or plaster your bag with stickers. That way, it'll be easier to spot.

11

Travel Trail Mix

What you need:

(gather some, or all, of the following ingredients)

- ½ cup raisins
- ½ cup dried fruit, like cranberries
- ½ cup peanuts
- ½ cup M&M's
- ½ cup yogurt-covered raisins or yogurt-covered peanuts
- ½ cup sunflower seeds
- 1 cup pretzel sticks or mini pretzels
- 1 cup Chex cereal

Utensils:

- Measuring cups
- Large bowl
- Wooden spoon
- Several small plastic bags

What you do:

Mix together all the ingredients in a large bowl. Then place a cup of trail mix in each plastic bag and pack your trail mix snacks to go.

Meltdown alert! If you're using M&M's or yogurt candies, don't leave your trail mix in the sun or in hot places (like locked inside a car). The chocolate or yogurt can melt, leaving you with a mess of a mix!

Hitting the Beach or Other Summer Hot Spots

For summer fun, don't forget to pack these essentials. *(Check out the fill-in travel list in the back of this book to make your own custom list!)*

 swimwear, plus a cover-up

 a beach towel

 sunscreen

 bug repellant

 flip-flops or shower shoes

a waterproof camera

 a beach bag

sunglasses

 a visor or straw hat

TRAVEL TIP

Trying to cram all you can into your suitcase? Try rolling your clothes instead of folding them. Not only will it help eliminate some of the wrinkles, but it will also open up more room for your stuff.

Ski Trips and Winter-Weather Getaways

If there's snow or cold weather in your vacation plans, be sure to bring along this cold-weather survival gear.

lotion

lip balm

boots

warm socks

hand-warmer packs

a knit hat

gloves with water-proof liners

long underwear or thermal underwear

a scarf or neck warmer

sunglasses

sunscreen (Winter's rays can be just as harmful as summer's!)

14

TRAVEL TIP

It's a good idea to bring extra clothes to wear in case the weather isn't what you expected. For instance, even though you're headed to a hot locale, it's smart to bring some long pants, a sweater or sweatshirt, and a light jacket, in case of a chilly evening. Or if you're off into the cold, bring clothing that can be worn in layers, like a jacket over a sweater that's worn over a T-shirt. That way, if it gets too warm, you can always peel off a layer or two.

Roughing It

Heading off into the great outdoors? Here are some essentials you definitely won't want to forget.

 a flashlight and spare batteries

bug repellant

 anti-itch cream for bug bites or poison ivy

a first-aid kit

hair scrunchies and ponytail holders

 a baseball cap

travel-sized packages of tissues

 a compass

a whistle

a water bottle or canteen

Summer Camp Special:

Wanna really be prepared for summer camp? Bring along these extras and you'll be ready for anything!

A backpack: It'll help you carry snacks, sunscreen, and more on those day-long hikes and excursions.

A bandanna: Wear it as a headband, a head scarf, a belt, or a carry-all. A bandanna will definitely come in handy and protect your hair while you're hiking through the woods!

A stationery kit with pens, paper, and stamps.

A disposable instant camera: Instant pictures to share? You bet! These cameras spit out photos in seconds. You can use them to send photos home or to decorate your bunk.

TRAVEL TIP

Don't forget to pack something nice to wear! Bring along a dress or skirt in case your vacation plans call for a fancy dinner or a last-night-of-camp dance.

Band-Aids: Between bug bites and brushes with prickly plants, you'll find that having Band-Aids on hand will save you a few trips to the camp nurse. (And you can always use Band-Aids as tape to stick photos to your bunk.)

Your favorite pillow: Having your favorite pillow with you will make sleeping away from home a little easier and a lot more comfortable!

A flashlight: Late-night bathroom trips and after-hours bunk fun make a flashlight pretty much indispensable!

TRAVEL TIP

If you're traveling by plane, be sure to pack at least one extra outfit, as well as toiletries like your toothpaste, toothbrush, and hairbrush, into the bag that you'll be carrying on board. You never know when your luggage might be lost!

17

Part 2

Fun for the Road: Entertainment, Games, and Crafts

Being stuck in your seat for a long period of time—whether in the car, a camp bus, or on a plane—can make you pretty restless unless you're prepped with a supply of fun activities. Sure, you can pass the time by asking, "How much longer?" every five minutes or counting the exits before you get there, but there are far better ways to make time fly. Here are some fun ideas, cool crafts, and super games to help you tackle travel-time doldrums.

Now That's Entertainment

There's loads you can do to keep yourself entertained while you're on the road or on vacation. Here are some ideas to consider.

Books

Vacation is one of the best times to read books just for fun! Head to the library, a bookstore, or on-line and get yourself a few good books to read on the road or at your destination.

Audiotapes

If you have a portable tape or CD player, you're in luck! There's lots out there for your listening pleasure. You can check out or buy books on tape or CD, and listen to them in your player or in the car's stereo. Or you can bring along some of your favorite music to listen to. You can also have friends record a taped message for you that you can listen to while you're away from home.

Travel Games

Portable travel games are made for taking on trips. They're small enough to take along, and often use magnets to keep all the pieces in place in case you run over an unexpected bump or hit a little turbulence. Here's a list of some favorite games that just happen to come in convenient travel sizes:

Backgammon

Battleship

Checkers

Chess

Connect Four

Memory

Scrabble

Sequence

Wheel of Fortune

Yahtzee

TRAVEL TIP

You can learn about your vacation destination and enjoy a good leisurely read at the same time by getting a book that's set in the same part of the country you'll be visiting. Ask your librarian to help you hone in on stories that are related to your trip.

21

Hand-held Games

The electronic era has arrived, and you can reap some of the benefits by getting your hands on one of these hand-held electronic games—perfect for your travels!

Frogger

Hangman

Mastermind

Monopoly

Trivial Pursuit

Nintendo Game Boy
(with its line of specially made games)

TRAVEL TIP

Great news for movie lovers: Some companies now rent in-car video players that hook up to the car's lighter! Just rent the machine, get your hands on a few good movies, and break out the popcorn for movies on the move! Point your parents to www.survivethedrive.com to find out about renting a video player for the ride.

Summer Camp Special:

Who needs Brandy or 'N Sync to make melodies at camp? So long as you have a few willing camp pals, you can start your own song fest, with or without the background music! Gather your friends together and come up with a theme song for your bunk, then sing it aloud when you're off on hikes together or when you're about to compete in camp contests. If you can get a hold of a tape recorder, you can record yourselves singing for everlasting memories!

Make Your Own Travel Games

Don't want to take up a bunch of space in your bag with entertainment stuff? These game suggestions are easy and only involve a couple of arts-and-crafts materials!

Travel Bingo

(Two or more players)

Have each player get out a piece of paper and copy down this bingo card diagram. Then fill in the blank boxes with different travel items from the suggested list on the next page (you can only use each one once). Now you're ready to play! As you see different things from your list, yell them out and mark them off on your cards. The first person who completes a row across, down, or diagonally yells, "Bingo" and wins the game.

Bingo Word List

Pay phone	Blue car	Yield sign
Motel	Hitchhiker	Person on a cell phone
Broken-down car	Eighteen-wheeler truck	Call box
Horse	Cement mixer	White car
Bumper sticker	Boat	McDonald's
Convertible	Out-of-state license plate	Fire engine
Storage facility	Barn	Motorcycle
Pine tree	Flashing yellow light	Orange construction cone
Cow	Police car	Rest stop
Trailer or motor home	Car wash	Personalized license plate

Triangle Game

(Two or more players)

On a piece of paper, draw rows of dots, with one dot in the first row, two dots in the second row, three dots in the third row, etc. Draw the dots to resemble a large triangle (see picture). The game begins with each player taking a turn by connecting two dots horizontally or diagonally, one line at a time. The object of the game is to connect dots to form a triangle. Once you have completed a triangle, put your initials in the center of it. When neither player can create any more triangles, count up your initials. The person who captures the most triangles wins!

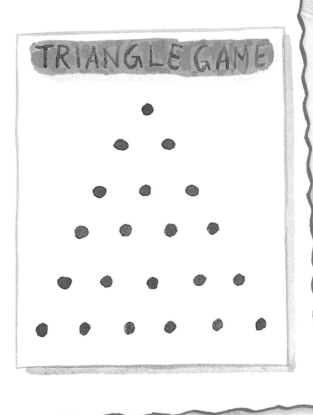

Word Games

P ass the time by testing your word skills. You can play with a friend or test yourself. You'll find the answers to all the games and puzzles in this section on page 45.

Trickle-down Puzzles

Change the word in the first line to the word listed in the last line, one letter at a time, using only real words. Remember: Each one can have only one letter changed from the word above it.

1. MOOD

    _____
    _____
    _____

    BARN

2. LEFT

    _____
    _____
    _____

    MIND

3. CAT

    _____
    _____
    _____

    TEN

Scrambles

Unscramble the following words that you're likely to encounter on a road trip:

1. AGS ITTNSAO _____

2. LOMTE _____

3. ALBODILBR _____

4. KURTC OSPT _____

Puzzlers

Figure out the hidden meanings in these verbal puzzles.

1. sandCHICKENwich

2. HEAD
   HEELS

3. C
   O
   U
   N
   T

4. the DANCING street

5. LIPS LIPS

6. us STOP

7. class IN class

Mind Stumpers

1. The following sentence has two gaps that can be filled in with two different words that use the same exact letters. Can you figure out the two seven-letter words?

The _____ felt lonely on the frontier and longed for _____ from home.

2. The answers to the following clues all rhyme with one another. Try to figure them out.

You can go up it or down it: _____

You get it when it's cold outside: _____

It won't be smaller than a dollar: _____

It's a kind of pickle: _____

3. Name each correct state by following the clues. Then use the first letter of each word in the answers to reveal a word that is what this book is all about!

It was named after Queen Elizabeth I.

_____

It's got a bunch of A's.

_____

It's the home of the Mile-High City.

_____

It's the farthest north.

_____

It's home to the country music capital.

_____

It's got a Windy City.

_____

Lewis and Clark ended their journey here.

_____

It's got a Big Apple.

_____

Secret Word

_____

4. Starting with the first letter in the first column, spell out a famous U.S. landmark by moving up, down, forward, or backward, but not diagonally, using each letter just once.

```
S T U

T A E

B I O

E L F

R T Y
```

[   ]

5. See if you can figure out the names of these movies, which are spelled below without any vowels:

TTNC [   ]

JRSSC PRK [   ]

NDPNDNC DY [   ]

SH'S LL THT [   ]

TH WDDNG SNGR [   ]

Word Search

Traveling by plane? If so, you'll be very familiar with the following words. Try to find these hidden air-travel terms in the word search puzzle below.

Airport

Gate

Jet

Pilot

Runway

Seat belt

Taxi

Ticket

```
T L R U N W A Y E A
R A I C K P J G A T
O P X W X T O L I P
P X T I C K E T E G
R T E T X P T T L K
I T L E B T A E S N
A L T J J F G B E P
L O P E T A F K G R
```

What Comes Next?

Each of the following puzzles shows a sequence—items that are linked in a certain order. See if you can figure out what letter or number is missing from the following sequences.

1. J F M
    A M J
    J A ?

2. A D G
    C F I
    B E ?

3. S S F T W T ?

4. 12 21 36 63 45 ?

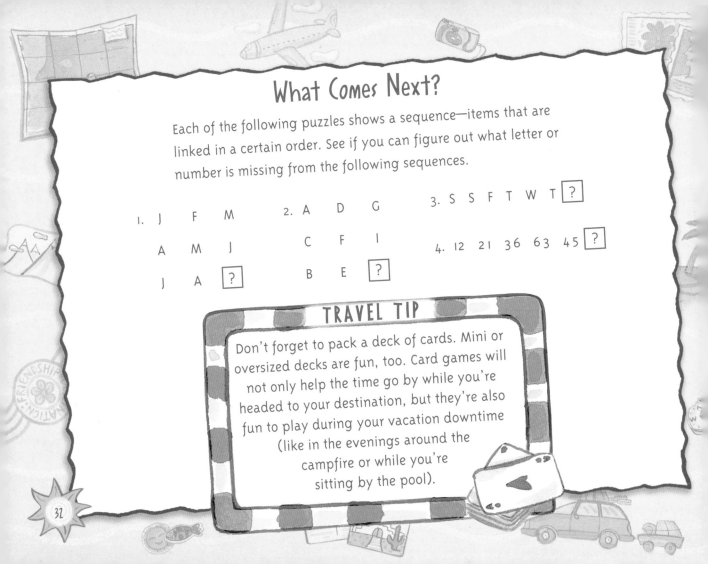

TRAVEL TIP

Don't forget to pack a deck of cards. Mini or oversized decks are fun, too. Card games will not only help the time go by while you're headed to your destination, but they're also fun to play during your vacation downtime (like in the evenings around the campfire or while you're sitting by the pool).

Brain Teasers

Spend some time trying to figure out these tricky brain stumpers!

1. The final score of a baseball game was 1–0, yet no man crossed home plate. How was that possible?

   _____

   _____

2. Two mothers and two daughters went shopping together, and each bought a pair of shoes. There were only three pairs purchased. How is that possible? _____

   _____

3. How is it possible for someone born on December 25 to always have her birthday come during the summer?

   _____

   _____

4. Ashley and Emma have the same parents. They were born on the same day and look exactly alike, yet they are not twins. How is that possible?

   _____

   _____

5. A girl kept asking the same question all day long. She got different answers to the same question, yet each answer was right. What was her question?

_____

_____

_____

6. Which is heavier—a pound of steel or a pound of feathers? _____

_____

7. Beth is older than Alexa but younger than Elise. Kara is younger than Beth but older than Alexa. Put the girls in order of their age, from oldest to youngest. _____

_____

_____

8. Where does Friday come before Wednesday? _____

Kooky Stories

Create funny travel stories by asking your family or friends to come up with different types of words to fill in the blanks. Once they've provided all the words to fill in the blanks, read the silly stories aloud. Here are two examples.

Crazy Postcard

Dear _____,
(name of someone you know)

Greetings from _____. The weather is_____, and the
(place)   (adjective)

sight seeing is_____! Yesterday, we ran into_____
(adjective)   (name of a celebrity)

playing_____. It was so_____ to watch. We also
(a sport)   (adjective)

visited this amazing restaurant named _____. I had
(a restaurant)

_____ and it was so _____ that I know I'll return.
(a food)   (adjective)

Next on our itinerary is_____. We'll be going by
(name of place)

_____ in _____ days. I'll send you a_____
(means of transportation)   (number)   (singular noun)

from there.

Love, _____
(your name)

My Vacation

This _____, I took a trip with my family to_____.
(season of the year)   (place)

We even invited_____along, too. I made sure to bring along a
(name of person you know)

_____, as I knew it could get pretty_____ that time of year.
(noun)   (adjective)

Before we left, I made sure to eat a _____ breakfast so that I
(adjective)

would be full of _____. Everything was going great until our_____
(noun)   (adjective)

car broke down in the middle of _____. What a _____! But
(place)   (noun)

then, of all things, _____ was driving by and stopped to help us.
(male celebrity)

I was so thankful that I offered to give him my _____. He said no thanks
(noun)

and told me I was quite a _____ girl. Wow! It definitely turned out to
(adjective)

be the _____ vacation I ever had!
(adjective ending in -est)

Summer Camp Special:

Create a friendship memories book using construction paper, a hole punch, and ribbon ties. Have your camp pals fill in their answers to each question (be sure to provide enough pages for all of your friends). Once they're done, add your thoughts, then share the book with all of your pals!

Name:.....................................

Nickname: ....

Counselor: ....

The best camp food is: ....

The camp food that's truly gross is: ....

Fave camp activity:.......................

Worst camp activity:......................

If you were head counselor, you'd: ....

Other campers will remember you for:........

What you miss most from home:..............

What you'll miss most about camp: ....

Getting Crafty: Ideas to Create

With a few basic supplies, you can make crafts just about anywhere—whether in a plane, train, log cabin, or car.

Pack Your Craft Bag

What to bring from home:

4"x 6" index cards
(great for making postcards)
colored pencils or pens
pad of paper
small pair of scissors
glue stick
stickers
colored construction paper

What to collect along the way:

brochures of towns or hotels
straws
maps
pinecones or other
items from nature
postcards
paper place mats from restaurants
toothpicks

Bookmarks

Create a cute bookmark by attaching stickers, or pictures from travel brochures you've collected, to a piece of cutout colored construction paper.

TRAVEL TIP

To really jazz up your crafts, get a pack of stickers that have to do with the type of trip that you're taking. For instance, if you're headed on a camping adventure, get stickers of camping-related items such as tents, fish, and campfires. Or, for a holiday trip, collect holiday-themed stickers.

Travel Calendar

Use this model to create your own trip calendar. Write in the dates, then fill in the boxes with info about the day, including where you were, how you got there, and what happened. Decorate it with stickers and drawings, or glue on mementos you've collected during the trip.

Postcards

Use blank 4" x 6" cards to create your own postcards to keep or send home to friends and family. Draw pictures from your trip on one side of the card, or glue on stickers or pictures or mementos from along the way. On the other side, draw a line down the middle of the card. Use one side to write your message and the other side to address and stamp the postcard.

Picture Frames

With all the shots of your vacation that you'll be capturing on film, wouldn't it be fun to create a frame to hold one special shot? Use colored construction paper as the base of your frame and use straws or toothpicks to create a border around the frame. Then decorate it with drawings, stickers, or items you've collected along your journey. You can also include the treasures of nature around you — gather flowers or pretty leaves if you're in the woods, or collect shells and sand if you're spending time at the beach.

Summer Camp Special:

What kinds of crafts are best at camp? Crafts you make with, and for, friends, of course! Bring along two-foot strands of colored embroidery string and safety pins, and follow these instructions to make super-cute buddy bracelets!

1. Take six strands of colored thread and knot the threads together at one end.

2. Stick a safety pin through the knot, and then fasten it to your shorts or something sturdy, like a heavy backpack.

3. Pull the threads apart from one another, and keep them straight and flat.

4. Take the first thread on the left (#1) and knot it onto the thread to the right of it (#2).

5. Then knot thread #1 to #3.

6. Continue knotting #1 onto the other threads, one at a time.

7. After you've finished that row, start knotting #2 onto #3 through #6, then finally to #1.

8. After you thread #6, repeat the process starting with #1. Keep going until the bracelet is long enough to fit around your wrist.

9. Then tie the bracelet on your friend's wrist. (If the ends are too long, borrow scissors from the camp's craft counselor to snip them off.)

Home Sweet Home

The thought of all your vacation fun coming to an end can be a bit of a downer, that's for sure. But try not to be too bummed that the trip is ending. After all, you'll have a whole collection of special memories to help you recall all the fun you've had, especially if you fill out the travel journal in the next section of this book! Besides, coming home does have its benefits—you get to see your friends again and share stories about your trip with them! Plus, being away from home for a length of time will give you a whole new appreciation for all the things you've left behind, like your room, your pets, and the rest of your family (if you're traveling without them). And don't forget—you'll have many more vacations to look forward to!

Answers

TRICKLE-DOWN PUZZLE, pg. 27
1. mood, moon, morn, born, barn.
2. Left, lift, lint, mint, mind.
3. Cat, can, tan, ten.

SCRAMBLES, pg. 28
1. Gas station; 2. Motel; 3. Billboard;
4. Truck stop.

PUZZLERS, pg. 28
1. Chicken sandwich; 2. Head
over heels; 3. Countdown;
4. Dancing in the street; 5. Tulips;
6. Stop following us; 7. In between
classes.

MIND STUMPERS, pg. 29-30
1. Settler, letters; 2. hill, chill, bill,
dill; 3. Virginia, Alabama, Colorado,
Alaska, Tennessee, Illinois, Oregon,
New York. Hidden word = vacation;
4. Statue of Liberty; 5. *Titanic,
Jurassic Park, Independence Day,
She's All That, The Wedding Singer*

WORD SEARCH, pg. 31

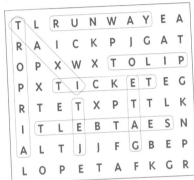

```
T L R U N W A Y E A
R A I C K P J G A T
O P X W X T O L I P
P X T I C K E T E G
R T E T X P T T L K
I T L E B T A E S N
A L T J J F G B E P
L O P E T A F K G R
```

WHAT COMES NEXT?, pg. 32
1. S, for September—the list follows
the names of months of the year;
2. H—each letter is the third letter
after the previous; 3. M, for Monday—
it's the days of the week, backwards;
4. 54—each pair of numbers has their
digits reversed.

BRAIN TEASERS, pg. 33-34
1. All the players were female; 2. The
shoppers were a grandmother, her
daughter, and her granddaughter;
3. She lives in South America, where
the seasons of the year are reversed;
4. Ashley and Emma are part of a
set of triplets; 5. What time is it?; 6.
They both weigh the same—a pound
is a pound!; 7. Elise, Beth, Kara,
Alexa; 8. In the dictionary.

45

Part 3

Making Memories:
Cool Ideas and a
Fab Fill-in Journal

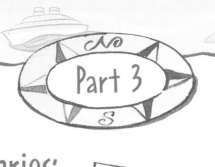

Y ou can savor all the great fun of
a vacation long after the trip is over!
Remember the good times you've had by
creating keepsakes you can hang on to forever.
In this section, you'll get a bunch of ideas for
keeping your vacation memories—plus a journal
to record your memories in.

Captured on Film

Taking pictures will ensure that you don't forget the great times you had on the trip. No matter where you're headed, be sure to pack a camera and plenty of film! Here are some tips to make sure the pictures you take are top-notch.

DO go for some candid shots of people, which means taking pictures that aren't posed. While posed photos are great, candid shots enable you to capture the action.

DON'T stay out of all the pictures. Ask someone else to get behind the camera for some of the shots so that you can make an appearance in your photo album, too!

DO get a little closer. Vary your vast scenic shots with close-ups. Go in close for a shot of a shell or a pretty running brook.

DO pay attention to lighting. If it's starting to get dark out, be sure that your flash goes off or turn it on manually.

😞 **DON'T** shoot directly into the sun. (You'll get a picture that's totally washed out!)

😊 **DO** encourage the people in your picture to keep their eyes closed until you say, "Cheese!" That way, they'll be able to show their bright, wide eyes just in time for the picture.

😊 **DO** hang onto the negatives of your pictures. That way you can have certain shots enlarged so you can frame them or you can make duplicates for your friends.

😊 **DO** consider going digital. If you have access to a digital camera, try using it to get shots that can be printed from your home computer or e-mailed to your buds.

Lights, Camera, Action!

Add a little action to your vacation memories by recording the trip on video or on audio. If you have access to a video cam, bring it along and tape the highlights of your trip.

No video cam? Get your hands on a tape recorder and narrate your trip on tape. Talk about the journey, places you are visiting, and your impressions of the things you are doing and seeing. Interview other people, such as family members on the trip or who you are visiting. Don't forget to record sounds from the trip, like water rushing in a river, waves crashing at the seashore, or all the commotion of a big city.

TRAVEL TIP

If you plan to record your vacation on video, be sure to bring plenty of blank tapes and the battery charger. At night, recharge the battery for the next day.

Wish You Were Here!

Just because you're away from home doesn't mean you can't keep in touch with your friends. Collect addresses and e-mail addresses from pals ahead of time — there's a handy address area at the end of this section to note them!

Here are some ways to send your regards from afar.

Postcards: Buy and send postcards from your vacation destination and stops you make along the way. Go beyond the basic "Having fun, wish you were here" greeting and instead write about the activities you are doing and the people you're meeting. You can also use the funky postcards included in this month's stationery pack!

E-mail: E-mail makes it possible for you to send messages to your pals, pronto! Either bring along a laptop, or find another place to get wired. Lots of hotels and even airport lobbies and stores offer Internet access for free or a small charge. If you're staying with friends or family, you might even be able to borrow their computer to send e-mail and check for mail that's been sent to you. In order to get your e-mail on the road, though, you'll need to have access to an Internet-based e-mail account. Web sites like hotmail.com, delias.com, excite.com, and yahoo.com offer free e-mail addresses and access, so if you don't already have an Internet e-mail account, be sure to sign up for one before you go!

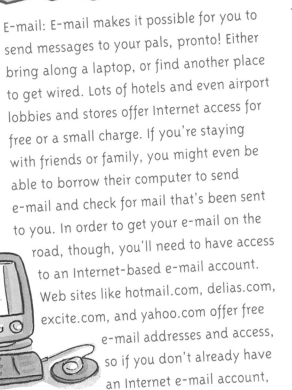

Telephone: Get a prepaid calling card before you go on vacation so that you can call friends or family. If you're headed to summer camp, or will be away from your family for a long period of time, you might want to have your parents look into getting a special 800 number that you can use to call them without having to spend a dime on your end.

TRAVEL TIP

Before you head out on your vacation, be sure to get lots of postcard stamps. That way, you can quickly and easily mail off postcards to friends and family.

Treasured Collections

A trip away from home is a perfect time to begin a collection of souvenirs from all different places that you can add to over time. Here are some ideas for a collection that you can start on your trip. (Try to find items that have the name of the town or location you're visiting on them.)

Baseball caps

Charms for bracelets

Flags

Key chains

Mugs

Pencils

Pens

Postcards

Posters

Refrigerator magnets

Rubber stamps

Shells

Snow globes

Souvenir spoons

Stamps

Stuffed animals

Thimbles

Ticket stubs

T-shirts

Traveling Teddy

Want a clever idea for a souvenir that you and your friends can enjoy? Consider buying a teddy bear and attaching a small notebook to him using a ribbon. Take him with you on your trip and record the dates and locations of your travels inside the notebook. Jot down special memories about the trip, like where Teddy spent the night or how he arrived at his destination. When you get home, pass along the bear and his travel journal to another friend who's headed off for vacation. She can read all about your travels and add her own stories. See how many spots Traveling Teddy can visit!

Summer Camp Special:

Wanna great way to collect all your camping buddies' autographs? Grab an old pillowcase, get a permanent marker, and let your pals sign their names and write a special camp memory on it. When you get home, place a pillow in the pillowcase and display your memories proudly on top of your bed. That way you can remember your summer at camp all year long!

My Travel Journal

ere's your chance to have some fill-in fun and record some memories. Use this travel journal to make vacation plans and write all about your travels. You'll also be able to enter special thoughts, memories, and keepsakes from every step of your vacation, from before you go to when you're headed home!

Vacation Planner

The date of my trip: ....

Where I'm headed: ....

How I'll get there: ....

Who's going: ....

Where I'll stay: ....

Things I'd like to do while I'm there: ....

....

....

....

Vacation Planner

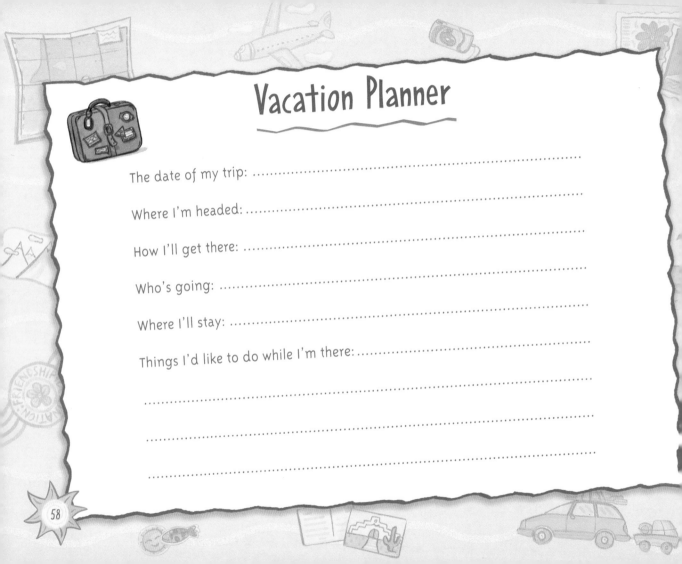

The date of my trip: ....

Where I'm headed: ....

How I'll get there: ....

Who's going: ....

Where I'll stay: ....

Things I'd like to do while I'm there: ....

....

....

....

Packing Checklist

Clothes

Use these handy lists to make sure you bring everything you need. Check off the items that you're taking on your trip. Write down how many of each item you should bring and cross off items on the list as you pack them into your suitcase or bag. There are also some handy fill-ins for any extra items you might need that aren't on the list.

jeans ____

dressy pants ____

casual pants ____

dressy dresses ____

casual dresses/ sundresses ____

skirts ____

shorts ____

short-sleeved shirts ____

long-sleeved shirts ____

sweatshirts ____

sweatpants ____

T-shirts ____

tank tops ____

sweaters ____

heavy jacket ____

lightweight jacket ____

raincoat ____

swimsuits ____

cover-ups ____

underwear ____

undershirts/bras ____

59

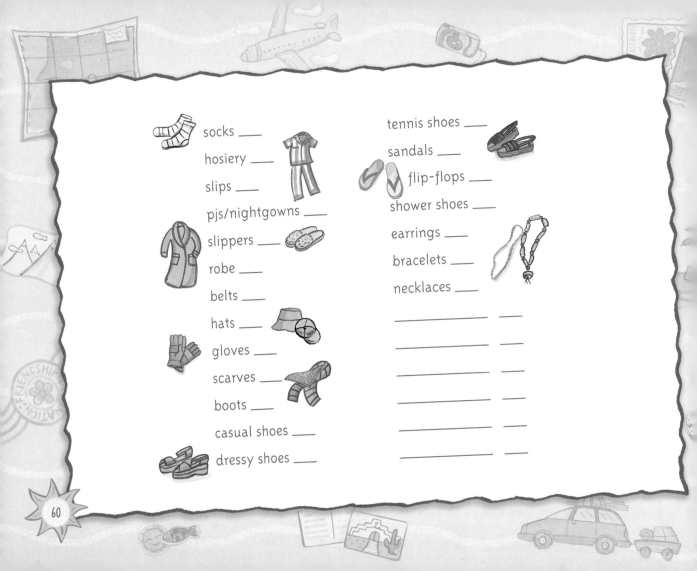

socks ____

hosiery ____

slips ____

pjs/nightgowns ____

slippers ____

robe ____

belts ____

hats ____

gloves ____

scarves ____

boots ____

casual shoes ____

dressy shoes ____

tennis shoes ____

sandals ____

flip-flops ____

shower shoes ____

earrings ____

bracelets ____

necklaces ____

_____ ____

_____ ____

_____ ____

_____ ____

_____ ____

_____ ____

Toiletries

shampoo ____

conditioner ____

hair gel/
styling products ____

hairbrush ____

comb ____

blow-dryer ____

curling iron ____

barrettes ____

ponytail holders/
scrunchies ____

headband ____

toothbrush ____

toothpaste ____

dental floss ____

soap ____

lotion ____

lip balm ____

tissues ____

sunscreen ____

fingernail clippers ____

file or emery board ____

nail polish ____

nail polish remover ____

cotton swabs ____

cotton balls ____

bug repellant ____

anti-itch cream ____

medication ____

bandages ____

first-aid kit ____

____ ____

____ ____

____ ____

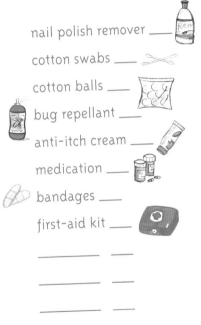

All the Extras

address book ___

backpack ___

beach towel ___

binoculars ___

books ___

camera ___

canteen/
   water bottle ___

film ___

flashlight and
   batteries ___

games ___

handkerchiefs ___

laundry bag ___

magazines ___

maps ___

pencils ___

pens ___

pillow ___

playing cards ___

portable radio ___

postage stamps ___

postcards ___

purse ___

sleeping bag ___

stationery ___

stuffed animals ___

sunglasses ___

swim cap ___

swim goggles ___

travel alarm clock ___

umbrella ___

watch ___

___ ___

___ ___

___ ___

___ ___

___ ___

___ ___

___ ___

___ ___

Roadside Finds

Record all the exciting stuff you came across on your journey, like cool stores you browsed in, road signs that made you laugh, restaurants and food that was definitely different from what you have at home, or special stops you made along the way.

....

....

....

....

....

....

Scenes from the Road

Use the following pages to attach pictures from your journey and things you collected during your trip (such as paper napkins from restaurants, matchbook covers, or postcards). Be sure to hang onto items like ticket stubs from museums or shows, plus the tickets from any bus, boat, or plane trips that you take.

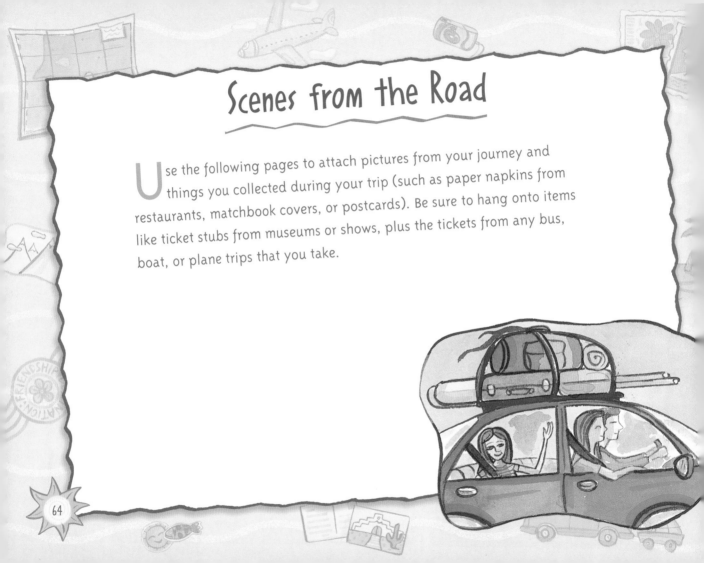

Travel Sketches

Use your artistic talent to draw pictures of some of the scenes from your trip here.

My Autograph Book

Create your own autograph book—a book full of messages from friends or people who you've met on your trip! Have them write a message to you, signing it with their name, the date, and where they're writing from, on the following pages.

Your Day-by-Day Diary

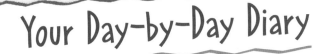

Photos, videos, and souvenirs are all great ways to save your travel memories. Another great way to remember all the fun stuff about your trip is to keep a travel diary. Use these pages to note stuff about your trip, including the places you've visited, the people you've met, and the sights you've seen.

Date: 12/26/13

Where I am: Reno/Circus Circus

Diary entry: It was so fun being there. I got a ton of tickets at the dropball game. Jackpot 15 times. buffet food was good, circus performance was cool and spending time with family was special.

Date: ....

Where I am: ....

Diary entry: ....

....

....

....

....

Date: ....

Where I am: ....

Diary entry: ....

....

....

....

....

Date: ....

Where I am: ....

Diary entry: ....

....

....

....

....

Date: ....

Where I am: ....

Diary entry: ....

....

....

....

....

Date: ....

Where I am: ....

Diary entry: ....

....

....

....

....

Date: ....

Where I am: ....

Diary entry: ....

....

....

....

....

Date: ....

Where I am: ....

Diary entry: ....

....

....

....

....

Date: ....

Where I am: ....

Diary entry: ....

....

....

....

....

Date: ....

Where I am: ....

Diary entry: ....

....

....

....

....

Date: ....

Where I am: ....

Diary entry: ....

....

....

....

....

77

Date: ....

Where I am: ....

Diary entry: ....

....

....

....

....

Date: ....

Where I am: ....

Diary entry: ....

....

....

....

....

Date: ....

Where I am: ....

Diary entry: ....

....

....

....

....

Date: ....

Where I am: ....

Diary entry: ....

....

....

....

....

Gone But Not Forgotten

Record your most memorable moments from your vacation here.

The best thing about the trip was: ....

....

My absolute favorite day of the trip was: ....

....

The funniest thing that happened was: ....

The best food of the trip was: ....

The worst food I ate was: ....

Someone who made this trip even more special was: ....

The most frustrating thing that happened was: ....

....

The friends I met during my vacation are: ....

....

If I could do this trip over again, I would: ....

....

....

....

....

Summer Camp Special:

My Summer Camp Journal

Camp Name: ....

Location: ....

Dates I attended: ....

My group name: ....

My counselor: ....

Why I chose this camp: ....

My favorite activity: ....

My best friends at camp: ....

....

The funniest moment of camp: ....

....

The best time I had was when: ....

....

My bunk mates, and where they're from: ....

....

The hardest part of camp: ....

My best day at camp: ....

....

Summer Camp Sign-Off

U se the following pages for autographs and notes from your friends at camp!

Don't Forget to Write!

Use these pages to keep the names and addresses of friends with whom you'd like to stay in touch while you're gone. Take their vacation address if they're going away, too. You can also add in names of friends who you meet along the journey or during the trip so that you can stay in touch once you get back home!

Name: Leta

Address: 5270 Rio Grande dr.

E-mail address: Karyrze@gmail.com

Telephone number: 405-677-6902

Name: ....

Address: ....

E-mail address: ....

Telephone number: ....

Name: ....
Address: ....
E-mail address: ....
Telephone number: ....

Name: ....
Address: ....
E-mail address: ....
Telephone number: ....

Name: ....
Address: ....
E-mail address: ....
Telephone number: ....

Name: ....
Address: ....
E-mail address: ....
Telephone number: ....

Name: ....
Address: ....
E-mail address: ....
Telephone number: ....

Name: ....
Address: ....
E-mail address: ....
Telephone number: ....

Name: ....
Address: ....
E-mail address: ....
Telephone number: ....

Name: ....
Address: ....
E-mail address: ....
Telephone number: ....

89

Name: ....
Address: ....
E-mail address: ....
Telephone number: ....

Name: ....
Address: ....
E-mail address: ....
Telephone number: ....

Name: ....
Address: ....
E-mail address: ....
Telephone number: ....

Name: ....
Address: ....
E-mail address: ....
Telephone number: ....

Name: ....
Address: ....
E-mail address: ....
Telephone number: ....

Name: ....
Address: ....
E-mail address: ....
Telephone number: ....

Name: ....
Address: ....
E-mail address: ....
Telephone number: ....

Name: ....
Address: ....
E-mail address: ....
Telephone number: ....